and other shores

Ian Stephen was born in the Isle of Lewis, Outer Hebrides of Scotland and has spent most of his life there. He began to share poems and stories, internationally, from his time at the University of Aberdeen. His first poetry collection was with Dangaroo Press, Denmark, 1983. *Adrift* was published by Periplum, Olomouc, 2007. Stephen represented Scotland in Canada as part of the Scottish Poetry Library's 2014 'Commonwealth Poets United' project, reading at Edmonton Poetry Festival. A new and selected poems 'Maritime' was published by Saraband in 2016. Recent poems in *Acumen, Magma, Poetry Salzburg Review, The Rialto, Stand.*

His film-poetry was included in 'Running Time' – Scottish Art Film, 2011, as well as being part of his work as first artist-in-residence at StAnza poetry festival and in the Czech Republic.

and other shores

Ian Stephen

Shearsman Books

First published in the United Kingdom in 2026 by
Shearsman Books Ltd
PO Box 4239
Swindon
SN3 9FN

Shearsman Books Ltd Registered Office
30–31 St. James Place, Mangotsfield, Bristol BS16 9JB
(this address not for correspondence)

ISBN 978-1-83738-023-7

CONTENTS

Positions

Fix
(for Saki)

So many tracks
in pencil or pixels
your own and the others.

Solid or dotted
erased or saved
screened or printed.

Foot treads
wakes
vapour trails –

it's the way
two transits become
one definite fix

if
there's an angle.

Tannara Mòr postage stamp project – Saki Satom

Skylight (circa 1980)
(for BZ)

I'm lying with you a mile inland
under rain that drills the roof-sheets
storms all chinks in the flashings.

The sealed window unit isn't.
There happens to be a power-cut
and there's a depth of singing height
above the weather.

We're not moored to
anything I've seen
sink or rise on a tested line.
We'll hold together tonight.

Skylight (circa 2020)

These clouds look steady enough.
Their sky anchors must be out
though I can't see the traces
of the cables
but the plough is on the move,
fair sweeping along.

You join up the dots
to catch the action.
The whole picture,
even the one in one window,
doesn't bother to wait.
A system drives itself
out of the skylight.

The constellation
hasn't got away.
The iron up there
tight on aluminium.
Polaris is further
out of the frame.

Lyrics for Sean and Rosie

Did you dwell here with me
in this beehive of placed stones
if only for summers
when cattle were heavy?

Did our barley-rigs hold
in deep-cleared furrows
between acidic turf
and the salted rock.

Did you bait lines for us
at the head of this steep loch
where Sròn Ulladale bears
to winter whitefish?

Will we set a fire now,
light it this ebb tide
to send out a signal –
heat smoke and hope.

Should we plant a rowan here?
The seed of red berries
for imagination
to germinate when
leaves mould, stars die?

A hawthorn for healing –
spur and leaf balm.
We should put a bit back
for others to find
at a possible later.

Rooting for ourselves
and for us all.

Adapted from lyrics in 'Malin Hebrides Minches' –
with photos by Sam Maynard, Dangaroo Press, 1983

Field notes

(Following William MacGillivray, naturalist and artist, 1796–1852)

1   Barabhas

you can put your hand to
this form in the rushes
still warm though

the speed of cooling air
snaps at your knuckles
but the smoulder
of this morning

will equalise temperatures
and the fog will be gone
like the hare

2   Gearrannan

treading the turf
Gearrannan, Dhail Mhor
looking to footfalls

wary of fleeing wolves
carrying their own young
on their eight legs

below us and them
the underswell
at Àird a' Ghobhann

which Smith
was he?

3   On Todun

a parent plover wades
deer-grass gold

a cuckoo in the scrub
of birch and myrtle

a merlin cuts across the face
of field-vole rock

so sharp
we expect
blood from stone

4   Pabaigh Mòr

a cistern in drystone
wetted by flood
now holds velvets

greens for the stab
of crabbing heron

5   Eadar Dha Fhadhail,

stark caps
small commons
stern wind
between two fords

6   Beinn Dhubh Losgaintir

Paul is a composer
who identifies birds
from their sounds
as well as their shapes.

'It could be in the modes or the key.
I haven't got perfect pitch.
I've faith in frailty.'

He had a brother he never saw.
Lost, over the grey brow
of this very ridge.

That's really
why we're here
where sundews
trap specks
with no noise
that we can detect.

A peregrine shadow
traverses from
moorland to foreshore.

A distinct wingline
then
a blur and shriek.

Don't forget
(For KC)

Don't forget
to send me a wave or two
from the other side.

Just dip
the pulse
in your long fingers
to the churn
of Manhattan.

It won't be instant
but of course I'll sense it
arriving in
at our own west side.

East side (Isle of Lewis)

It's only one clear line
one of the unwritten rules
between the sharp upper shape
and the lower

probably

a reflection.

In this light now
the rocks in air and water
are strong white equal.

The little green's gone.
Maroon's a tint –
garnet in tide-damp greys.

A stubborn hair that's blonde
(For MC)

I   *A calm*

Life in town is quiet between the gusts.
I'll need to sneak out,
gather the polystyrene shapes
left by the last squall.
But there's remnants
inside as well as out.

Like a stubborn hair that's blonde
on the black of my gansey.
And I'm not in a hurry
to tidy that one up

so I'll remember
the tangle and fankle
the craic and cackle
when your mane got caught
in the stainless ring
in my ear.

2   *It's the back of 3*

The dance beat's going next door
and my head's south but
thinking back to when we
found ourselves north
at the foot of our bed.

That time we did meet
the warm moor
seeped oil
up to feet.

Now there's another
recollected sense.
It's in a Lewis western
at the start of the priest's glen
and there's a clatter
of distant firing
– a Gatling gun –
but it's your lips on my face.

3   On the wrong side

I'm on the wrong side of Loch Ròg,
casting from the high pier
to the black water
and I don't think squid's the bait
that you'll sense downtide
and I don't think
the thornback ray
are all that lie between us now.

Looking to the loom of Suaineabhal.
I know your home is snug
between the salt wrack and
that high watershed.

It would take more than a GPS
more than a spinning log
more than any monitor of
depth or altitude
to measure the closeness
between us now.

Beauly Firth

A whooper swan crouches white
in a field of short green shoots.

A girl lets her hands fall to her sides
holding tack
as a brown horse sprints away.

A white-ish pony wears
a grey-ish coat

wades in a pool
that was still.

It's no epic
Dingwall – Inverness

and east but this
is another western.

I don't know any more
what's wind, what's water.

It's all navigable
to the community of birds,
wading or walking.

Monument, Sutherland

At Bonar Bridge,
haar going threadbare.
Interference is already
burned-off all the
greysmoke saltflats.

A plaid of cloud
sent from the west of
the province of Sutherland
confuses contours.

There he is now
in tall Romance but
rodded to his column.
Stay there,
presiding silly
over Golspie Gala:
wheelbarrows driven in drag
towards heavy refreshments
in the marquee. A tall PA
pulsing bass.

Stay there, duke,
head to hurricanes.
Just one change –
go bald, thatchless.
Conduct
the lightning.

Caithness

The sun is hitting out
from under the northerly

so a pale boat bobs
a tad brighter

than the white horses
on the bight

– they're 'white rabbits'
to my pal Saki.

Clouds close ranks
as we make the turn

to shoot
the funnel of the Strath.

The direction of sleet
 is always at you.

A first line of hills
is smudged.

There's nothing but
precipitation

then mitigation
in greys.

That Whistler should have got his arse
up this railroad.

North Coast

(for AP)

Russet up there,
thick to the roots of it

but even Sutherland
turns the corner

Tongue and Eriboll
Portskerra

till that east-going stream
stalls off the rocks at Mey

– a ceasefire of slack
till the tide gets a grip

makes a run at
the coming weight from west

wind and swell
hurtled from Greenland
with our salmon.

River physics

a log of canoeing the Spey: Insch Marshes to Craigellachie

I

The riven house stark
high above undercuts.

Sandmartins dart to
multistorey burrows.

Scouring and deposition –
 the physics of the river:

cobles shed high
as a flood falls

sand dropped later
and, lastly, silt.

When water bounces
you've two choices –

suspect a stray boulder
or put it down to volume

causing drops
to reach for air.

2

This night's water
fetched from the Feshie –
a river fallen
from a fossilised delta
that's out of eyeshot.

A while back
glaciers peeled off
the Scorran hills so
millions of gallons
hit a Spey
ten times bigger than
anything we'll see.

Tonnes of solids
would be carried
till meltwater lost
most of its energy.

A Strathspey is trickier than a jig.

A Strathfeshie would call for
fingering and breathing,
fore and stern rudder,
reverse ferrygliding
and the hearts of the dancers.

In the remains of a river
material is rounded.
Once these were
jagged offcuts.

3

Conversation occurs in eddies,
hung over with alder
cropping stray lures
by Abu, Svängsta.
A river's own
twisting economy.
Selling time.
Calling it sharing.

The Minch hornpipe
on a boat-grade whistle,
stable material unadorned.
But our plastic vessels
have a brace in ash.
Harmonicas out
from the poets' boat.
Tom's blues and the darting Gerry.

> 'There are three unequal spans of
> 25, 45, 80 feet
> and the deck is on a slope.
> This has been necessitated
> by the lie of the land,
> for there is a steep rock cliff
> on the south side but
> alluvial bank on the north.'

A ceilidh of construction
as the Eriskay love-lilt
comes to us via
Marjory Kennedy-Fraser
and the Glasgow Orpheus Choir.
The Spey provides crackle
and simulates the hiss
of approx. 78 RPM

4.

Harp on the lawn
jams with teabread,
powers into tight
vernacular phrasing.
We look to the bridge –
humane engineering
left in the wake
of barbarous redcoats.

           'D 1754
           E COMPANIES

           OF THE 33RD REG
           IMENT OF TH RIGHT
           HONOURABLE LORD
           CHARLES HAY
           COLONEL
           ENDED'

We lose the Cairngorms
when we lose the twang
spoken in uplands
when banking is mowed
when paddlers push on
to sniff for the brackish.

5.

Sodden studies
emerge from a drybag
with a ruined camera.
Capsize seepage
expresses itself
on paper holding
cloth and metal.
A matt mirror
for all these traces
of kindred settlement.
You know the important.
Cling to it
like sudden friendship.

But we're slow in drizzle and
allow the piper in our midst
to drive away to his next engagement.
Hawthorns at Black Boat Station
decorated with our own debris.
A Strip-The-Willow
the length of the platform,
to the dancer's diddling,
brings sweat over cold.

6.

We've to read rapids.
Find our own lines

There are no bearings
to take a long boat through
a short dog-leg.

Use our own bodyweights
to restore stability.
Conversation for buoyancy.

Sea-lice still hold
to migrating backs
under our boatskins.

7.

We sprint for malts.
Dorothy at Craigellachie
nods to Alistair's
whistled time,
holds your hand,
remembers herself
in the Speybay span,
most warm days
before embarking
for Alexandria.
Right there, across and back,
it was wide enough.

Five fish

(To be sung to the music of David P Graham)

1

This one seemed to be happy up there
sipping flies down to
her very own stones.

One day she fell with the current
all the way to the wide sea.

And then she was hunting shrimps and krill,
all that pink sinking in deep.
Tight muscle, slim as a rocket,
shine broken with flecks of black.

Till she and her mates turned around
thirsty for remembered water
flowing down into
brackish bights

so she swam until
her belly was bruised,
her shape remembered
in the gravel.

2

This one plays the water like air.
The high fin is long and a sail
so it swims in a spiral.
As a cork is unturned
from the cloudy neck

of a thick bottle.

The silver of salt
in fresh water.
The one that livens up when
the slowing chill is on the river.
She carries that useless fin of fat
but her spawning is out of kilter.

3

This dart is certain and sharp
but has fifteen spines
on its back.

You can see through shape
to hairy bones as
they bristle inside.

4

This one hovers,
striped by reeds,
like a shark in a lake.

He's made of marble
and gorgonzola.
Heavy as butter.

Pivots like a stuntbike
and rhymes with one too.

5

This back can show a kite
filling, pulling
round quiet water.

A tiger in olive and green
accelerating to
a flash of lipstick red.

1. salmon 2. grayling. 3. 15-spined stickleback. 4. pike. 5. perch

Orientation

The lay of the land

Lewisian gneiss was edged, down-ocean.
Durness rocks continue at St John's.
Our islands haven't shifted for a while

but our orientation
changes from year to year,
like compass variation.

We've got history from before Bannockburn –
navigators in boats of skin,
architects of chambered cairns.

The stepping stones are skewed.
We sail from Tamnavay by Skara Brae.
A course to Muckle Flugga, Faroe, Westmann.

Our dyes dare deep to saturation.
We tether visitors to cliffs or
bounce them out to archipelagos.

Our future is
dependable as damp
irregular as waves.

Like our shuttles,
our multiplaited lines
running
our own palms.

From a great circle – Nunatsuak

It's just too easy, this high –
you see snakes awake
as rivers get on the move.
Nunatsuak in
bare naked light.
The fraying runs
in a teal weave of terrain
have to be
a weft of waters.

In our recycled air
aperture is sensed,
shutter speed set.
You touch the screen
for exposure.
Nothing's square now,
down below,
except when we see it
within the corners
of our framing tools.

And these visible edges,
parallel for so long,
have to be
a human road,
no-go until the thaw.

There's an intersection,
on the ground
under our altitude,
more of a saltire
than a crucifix form.

How can you say
which is the major highway
with right
on its side?

Interior – Grain elevators

We don't see new blood at *Young*.
A long mustard shingle
sways on its single nail,
a swithering vertical
on slats gone to skin –
composing a cross
to the unknown farmer.

Watrous has a red tiled roof.
Lettering in oxide
on zinc sides, gone matt.
They say the settlement has a dancefloor
floating on horsehair
to absorb the stresses of the jigs.

At *Stalwart*
a transparent hawk
is airborne
with the shape of a vole in its beak.

They say the volunteers
from the great plains
went into the navy.
They could cope with space
which looks like nothing
to city-bred men.
They marched around
a mast in a field.

They went away.
Some came back.
Liberty
of a sort.

Lakeside 1– Kisiskatchewanisipi

Like the lark,
you hear before you see.
Unlike the lark,
'a low loud musical rattle'.

Like the greylag,
they cross the sky in number.
Unlike the greylag,
they don't hold a V for long.

Like starlings,
they gang in a bunch.
Unlike starlings,
they paint their wings with thermals.

Like ourselves,
they're brownish before grey.
Unlike ourselves,
they fuel up on frogs.

sandhill cranes

Lakeside 2 – Sweat Lodge

(for Louise Halfe and Peter Butt)

Grasses and grains
don't so much bend
as sway, crisp,
jutting over
misted ice.
The bits that were water
a few days back
are now less white
than the sections
which stayed solid.

Yesterday, man, dog
and a prancing coyote
did their dances in turn
on the frost-baked crust
over a suspension.
The character of melting
is different every day.
You can't clock the movement.
You can't see the greening
of sweating grasses
under their blanket.

You don't usually get to see
rocks walk but
yesterday I witnessed
a counted order of stones
go to crackle in ashes.
Each one went white
then turned to red
in the pit of our lodge.

Today I know
big rocks move too
even though they're slow.
Grandfathers, grandmothers –
they lost their hurry.

Waternames

In train-time
giving way to freight
you roam waternames –

Bad Lake, Luck Lake,
Big Stick Lake, Carrot River.
Old Wives Lake, Deception Lake,
Cold Lake, Lost Lake.

Knee Lake, Ear Lake,
Black Birch Lake, Timber Bay.
Dipper Lake, Bittern Lake.

Flatstone Lake, Smoothstone Lake,
Big Sandy Lake,
Big Muddy Badlands.
But

was land and water
taken
with the title?

South and North

Tales of Brave Ulysses
(I M Brian Johnstone)

The cellist came out of the academy
to lay down his melodies
when rhythm was on the line,
only one of his crimes
delivered at a pace
on the upright bass
not all that tender
on the six string fender.

The baker walked out of the jam
till the cake was cut with Cream
congealed.
How many rope-ladders
over the bearded rainbow
would it take
to touch the moon
sure as Armstrong?
Only one –
if it was long enough
and it was.

The lyrics of fate
over four strings
sounding like eight
syncopating
the pounding heat
from the baker back on the job,
so no-one was robbed.
A guitarist just in the lead
by a narrow neck.
The three-piece

gone off the rails
but in the groove
of spinning vinyl –
Corrievreckan
in technicolour.
Shipwrecks of
wailing bluesmen.
A stumble ashore
rolling and tumbling
casting out chords
like shining barley
on a slick of honey.
A parley with the shadows
of bottle-neck heroes
and music-hall maestros.

The set of wheels
went on fire
but your covered wagon
stitched its way
across its prairie
to elegy.
A fabric
picked and unpicked
by the pricking apostrophes
of Penelope
and the tailor
you had to sing to
so his paraffin
vaporised
in the hurricane.

Many's the riff went
over the cliff.
Jack, one hell of a lad,

a banshee mourner,
tall-story teller
but a master-mariner
when all the breezes
were out
of the ministry of bag.

Jack Bruce, Ginger Baker and Eric Clapton formed the band, Cream. The album title *Disraeli Gears* came from a roadie's slip of the tongue for a derailleur. *Tales of Brave Ulysses* was written by Clapton and Martin Sharp and sung by Bruce.

Songs for a Tailor (1969), with lyrics by Pete Brown, included *Rope Ladder to the Moon, Theme for an Imaginary Western* and *The Ministry of Bag*.

Bruce is credited with *Over the Cliff* on his 1970 album *Things We Like* (with John McLaughlin, Dick Heckstall-Smith and Jon Hiseman). He also played on the title track of the 1974 Frank Zappa album *Apostrophe (')*.

The tailor's house was often the ceilidh place because he picked up tales on his jobbing travels and there had to be a bright light (Tilley-lamp or perhaps a 'hurricane' lantern) to see his stitches. 'How many ladders to reach the moon?' is a recurring riddle in stories carried by travelling people.

For 'Ted', in Hobart

Vocal traces alternate,
amplitude and frequency
offset, coincide,
like and unalike
as bits of glacial ice
let loose in
a field that is not infinite
and has numbered days
of northbound mass.

Ted's tones are tuned
from ninety-one winters,
my own from fifty-nine.
She's content with
her hearing-aids
while I just lean in
to our tennis of vowels –
Tasmanian to Leosach.

It's me recalls the taste
of her campfire stew
made in Scotland.
A teacher exchange
when other Aussies
had to side with the States
on Vietnam.

Nothing scientific but –
Ted said she could never
reproduce the woodsmoke taste
even a day or two later.
Not even after other camps.
Not over there,
not back here.

Lunawanna Allonah

The curve of the long beach
faired to a sickle of bone.
Whitened. Like Losgaintir

but – a bounty of differences.
Funnel-red in the neb
of the black swan.

Lighter strips in the underwings
of the slow sea-eagle.
Eider shades in cormorant.

The strongest blue bobs
in the high tail of the male
'superb fairy-wren'.

The arching back of the echidna,
reversing out of a burrow –
a mammal that births a dome.

Nature isn't warped. Is what it is
though the story is that one quoll
was nibbled to claw and tooth

by the long mouths of its own tribe
through the mesh of
a humane trap.

The human species is the strange one.
Nothing irrational in the fear
of the Nuennnone people –
unburned bones

to be poked at
and stared at

for year after turning year.
At last the freckled ash
is on the warm north wind.

Gordon River

(for Randall Morrison)

As the wraiths pass,
a scroll of swatches –
graduations all
of a general green.

From this deck
the range of visible foliage
seems near enough to
shades of our own tufts
up in the old Hebrides.

But here, myrtles don't lie low.
They stretch for nutrients
up to high damp and
down from their buttress.

Whatever the hemisphere,
flora or fauna,
you see only what you see.
I'm with a sawmiller
on his day-off.
He points out the shoots –
portbottle green
an indicator of
a fallen Huon Pine.

But who can judge the extent
of birdseye speckling
within oiled yellow timber
built tight
from slow years

till the carcass is split.
Who knows what seams
you may find
when you open
a sassafras burr –
veins of blackness –
not spoiled but spalted.

It's our own features
we see as defects,
no longer latent.
Randall and me
compare the scars
on our palms –
our lists of operations
on the contractures
that will make claws of hands,
feet too, if we live long enough.

*Dupuytrons contacture, also known as a Viking badge –
an inherited syndrome*

Bruny Light

The convicts placed the stones to plan
till the tower was all it needed to be
to mark D'Entrecasteaux Channel.
One flash in twenty seconds,
as the clockwork turned,
the keepers logging on.
Wicks trimmed to spare the sperm-oil.

Looking out over The Friars,
a terraced garden
contained by hot stones
but death didn't run to order,
age or rank,
as it plucked the bairns
from cliff or bunk.

Up the slope,
the seeds that nobody planned
to leave in the ground
under lettering.
A picket of frail white slats
crosses a saturated blue,
deflects roaring forties.

Keening mothers,
wives to the keepers of this light,
hard earned their half-fathoms.

On Ocean Beach

The wavetops are dorsals.
Sideways on.
Individuals but
shoals of them.

They each flex
as if it is
the last stretch
of the membrane
that joins the rays
of the fin.
Living lacework.

Then the dory,
or dragonet,
gurnard, flathead
– the ones that seem to wear
their spine as spines

on top of their backs

– they fall as if they'd spawned
or spilled milt
into the shape
of the incoming wave

until the repercussions
of receding surf
become bandicoots
of froth.

A sampler of creeks

Stone Haven Creek –
the sign said.
Once, I bided by the Cowie Brig,
came to ken the town
as Stanehive.

The script may not imply
the thing that's said.
Take Findochty
spoken like
Finechtie.
There's maybe a double
down this way.

A whole history of association
in Black Bob's rivulet.
A border collie of that name
in the journals
of D C Thompson
in the city of Dundee.

But you'd need a long paddle
to point to the sources
of all surviving names
on the road to Strahan –

Scarlet Creek
Cardigan Creek
Patrolman's Creek
Raglan Creek
Snake Creek
Cemetery Creek

Maybe the last or first
has a claim
to speak for all –
Conglomerate Creek.
But every fissure in this land
has its own smudged syllables
– language spoken by no-one.

I'm thinking of a dusty Miller
a hemisphere up
and a few decades away.
In 'View From The Bridge'
his longshoreman says,
'How can I live without my name?'

from the log of 'Silver Moon', Jul/Aug 2025

Interlude in Húsavík

Maybe there are inherited names
in all our havens
like 'Peace and Plenty' –
for those who lost sons
– mothers stepping into
a perpetual fog, fathers
with no stories they can tell.

We catch, kill, fillet all we can eat,
sail in to capelin carnage
– tern darts, spitfire fulmar
and building tiers of broaches
– destroyers of white-beaked dolphin,
circling squadrons of minke,
heavyweight blows, backs, tails,
open feeding mouths of humpback.

A berth where hosepipes run forever.
Birds dive in their own efficient ways
– Shahed Arctic skua drones,
paravaning puffins.
We are taken to family feasts.

Our reunions must make mention
of the ghettoes of Gaza
where sacks of wheat are bait,
Think on the penned, the thirsty.
'Go here. Go there. Now.'

'perfect peace'
(Arctic and Northern Waters pilot)

Hesteyrarfjörður (66 20 N 22 51 W)

waterfall brushstrokes
bending below surface line
force 6 on forecast

white shines through particles
90 and counting whooper swans

Bhatasgeir – and other shores

(This section is dedicated to Ben Ziehm Stephen, drummer by trade, on the occasion of his passing out as a Royal Engineer, his first steps towards helping remove some of the world's ordnance.)

Just when you're ready to think

Just when you're ready to think
you've noted enough
of the endless variations,
never patterns,
drawn in sands
between a tide and another,
eyes are arrested again.

Effects are particular.
Drawings generate themselves,
get made, audience or no.
And it wasn't a sealpoint pencil
and it wasn't a few strands
of an otter's tail.

A gale-brush was involved,
wind, not water,
strong enough to recompose
plastered-down surfaces.

Impossible weight of wet
storm-sifted
as though it were dry stuff
and all our own
efforts to print
offset or intaglio
silkscreen or photo-gravure
are now seen to be
hesitant.

Messages

There are no messages
in the calligraphy of abandoned wire.

No containment now
even when the bendings cross.

More often,
the snapped bits waver.

The thicknesses
alter

like serifs
in a lost language.

Fencelines

(from the photography of Colin Myers)

1

The skeleton of our island
is high-tensile wire.
It's the struts
that make us viable,
ratcheted
over our disruptions,
cuttings and blastings
and planted dimples.

2

One guy's declining
is another's reclining –
the fenceline's ribs
greying on.
A line, tight once,
falls to a belly.
On Lewis
you might expect a fence
to look like a boat.

3

At the corner of a croft
a stone can point a finger
to an alignment
that might happen,

star or moon, when
the cloud is shoved aside
from that shallow saddle
in the now visible hill.

4

This notation
is sheepswool on rylock,
signed by the spun
balls and wisps,
familiar and foreign
as the singing and pausing
of Mary Smith,
Ishbel Macaskill.

5

A circle is impossible
in wire in wind.
Triangles of rock
are not really
that shape either.

Eilean Nèimh (On Nave Island, west Islay)

Bluebell and bracken and goose-shit.
A flock has flown
like dandelion down –
time gone on the gales.

A gable, still upstanding,
stones locked in lime.
A brick chimney juts
up from the inside

still holding it together –
a buttress in reverse
in a structure charted
as a chapel

though the labouring
shadows of kelp-burners
drag and fork to make
Eilean Nèimh pay.

We're not alone after all.
I sniff at tumbled creels
consider making one from two
but the gulls have got there first.

A bundle of speckled down
broken free by its own beak.
Beads watch me
back off.

In response to Orasaigh/Oronsay
by William Neil

Örfirisey – *approach from north*

Aye Willie we were were well out of The Bull Hole
– those jolts on the cable when tide stalled.
We came out the Sound. Reefed. Braced.

Shot from a catapult, Torran Rocks breaking to port.
Listening for Dubh Artach, blind to starboard.
You wouldn't think Colonsay could be so long.

Not risking our keel on the satellite crags,
we took the long way. Then inside the green caps.
A whistle of warp. Made fast, off the priory.

Orasaigh – *approach from south*

No keel on a currach. Oxhide fair slides
and Caol Ìle gives you quite the shove,
Buinnahabhain way back in the wake.

The great navigator gave us plenty choices
but we'd want a pilot to get her through the narrows.
Our prayers do not yet grant that clarity.

So it's west across the open stretch
and the flood will up her
to oyster, clam and the whiff of faith.

The Bull Hole is an anchorage off the Sound of Iona

Aquaculture
(from the photography of Colin Myers)

I.

A sky-spar is angling
to suspend the circus
of mesh cord and cringle
in courlene and nylon
polyprop and galv
– net on net but
no safety in it.

2.

Time was
the salmon was the bait
and the seal the one sought
but only the values
have shuffled in time –
it's still all about
meat and fat.

3.

The herring that were countless
are thin on the water
but gill-sized mesh
was cotton darkened
by oak-bark or cutch
and the lead ropes
were stretched high
along with wings of flax
– between
machair and cumulus.

4.

Cordage, they say,
has its memory but
is it really feasible
that all these skirts
of stretched meshes,
petticoats of synthetics,
can remember the currents
that shaped them
and fankled them
in turn?

5.

Thig a-steach an seo.
Come in close.
Coorie in by.
The knot made tight
by hand or machine
looks the same.
Who can say
if it's keeping out
spurdog and seal
or seeking to enclose them.
Either way
there's ones that got out
and in.

6.

Can there be visual echoes
– stakenets, bagnets, anchor and coble?
Even though the *salmonidae*
are thin in the water,

often lightweight now
and worth more when they snatch
at a General Practitioner,
Cascade or the traditional
Thunder and Lightning.
Then set free
in hope of spawn.

7.

It's strung,
suggesting a circle.
Can we avoid
a bent for curvature?
This net
was made round
in the first place.
Migrating fish
know their lines.

Elegant ellipse

(for the late Calum 'Stealag' Macleod)

To some, that's a circle squashed
– a bit like
the magnetism of
the sun and the earth
over a year.
The trickery is
a figure of eight.

The Aztecs knew the score
rediscovered
by Calum Macleod
son of John Macleod
blacksmiths both.
I was young when
I met the elder.
Lucky that
for I witnessed the younger
draw an elegant ellipse,
chalk on steel,
in a dance with
practical purpose.

A new mountain

Christine said, 'There's a new mountain.'
As if Sutherland changed overnight.
That hill-line does as all do
but we don't usually see the wear and tear
unless rocks become quarry.

Can't say why
cloud-cover comes in eights.
Can't grade visibility as one beholder
though you see the line go
from sharp. Back to the wash
before near-erasure.

Christine says 'smirr'
when mist and drizzle merge
to smudge
Suilven and Canisp
over Tiumpan Head
though a Minch away.

Today is different.
Some refraction replaced the mountains
with a new single shape, mild and more rounded
like it wasn't just weather
but had been weathering a while.
I thought of Mariupol.
That shape also changed.
Now looks like Aleppo.
They won't be restored
any time soon
in any change of light.

Starvation in the dust
of Gaza City.
Blood's drained or
dried on lime.
Bones are resilient
even as splinters.
Souls change status to 'lost'
even when directed
to places
on trains, trucks, ships.
Even when herded.

I M Alexander Hutchison, 1943–2015
author of *Gavia Stellata*[*]

You were an egret with all the time and whites in the world,
a lyric span, Clais Charnach to Vancouver,
a voice like a blackbird with a Buckie twang,
a memory for texts and students' names.

I'm sure I'm seeing your friend in Mol Mòr Bhatasgeir.
There's no red in the throat of sleet and hail
up to bust the curl of the surf-break.
She uptilts her beak with attitude then dives.

[*]*In* Bones and Breath *(Salt Publishing, 2013)*

As the crow flies

If the great crest of a grebe
is flattened by winter
and the ruddy throat
or charcoal patch
in distinctive divers
fades to a mottle,

if a merganser,
probable red-breasted,
is as far out of sight
as last year's autumn,
any identification
is inconclusive
as the impression
of a bruising shoulder of grey
in the peregrine arrow
driving down the saltings
as the crow flies.

If a six really did
turn out to be nine
as Jimi proposed
would it really matter
most of the time
as you watch what you see –
a merlin maybe
harries the sparrows
or redwings.

I M John Anderson
(Round-the world sailor and glider pilot)

I.

Eyes as bright as glints of gabbro
glanced from anchorage at Sgathabhaig
you both shone fresh as a new pin
out from the sail-repairer's tin.
It was Helen's stitches kept your arses
in the going-ashore shorts
that maybe started life as longs.

Practical as tacks of ribbed bronze –
a stitch in time to keep the deck on.
Plenty of the other sort of tacks
edging you off lee-shores,
ones you heard but never saw.
Your dacron cloth, crisp once,
might get recut
for tradewind jibs.

It was never about bigness –
no forty-footer to get you on the road.
You said the only thing scaled-up
 in the scantling of the Halcyon 27,
was the diameter of the wires,
tensed to carry small material wings.
that were to carry you –
Rathlin East Light to starboard,
whitewashed to its black bandana,
a painted rim like the sunburned neck
of the Commissioner of Irish Lights.
Shining out for all, no exceptions.

And then it was the letting go
to work your threadbare way
the whole way round
till you cleared that light again, to port.

2.

When it came to power propulsion,
to keep the show on the waters,
at least a summer migration,
wee blue *Mara* was sufficient
to nudge into berth sixty-nine
out of the North Minch chop.

And you would cross the bar to Soyea harbour
to document the transit
and unlikely archaeology –
ghosts of basking water-gliders
by seized machinery wanting oil.

The corridor to Na Garbh Eileacha –
a way into a monastic city
partially submerged in turf.
Haven for the living and the dead.

3.

When the seas were just too much
John looked back to the thermals
that pressed on flap and rudder,
when his finger was on a joystick
best foot on a pedal,
floating on trust.

But you both would cross to one of the world's ends
to count and log migrations –
wireless ones.
It takes a big man, slim John,
to sense such kinship
in those tiny navigators,
instinct in the vessels of their skulls
and never a twig
in a beak
or any other trace of calculations.

Soyea harbour – site of basking shark fishery and processing plant (Tex Geddes and Gavin Maxwell) Na Garbh Eileacha or The Garvellachs – see John's photo in Clyde Cruising Club/Imray Pilot notes. See also multiple articles in yachting press by Helen Anderson.

Surf-break, *Mol Mòr Bhatasgeir*

In that light which tends with easterlies,
the mainland silhouette, northways till it stops.
That would be Cape Wrath
by implication
and so we decipher
the species by what's noticeable –
the eider duck because a drake is near,
 the breast of withered red
because the punk crest shakes
on the dipping merganser.
A diving duck resists its name
by a shrug of drab
broken by a single lighter ring –
scoter, scaup or goldeneye but

what we always see on Mol Mòr is
polyprop and silicon in the tangle
– a debris jettisoned
in proportion to the enterprise.

We don't see but we know
our beads and beads remain in suspension
even in the clean-seeming roll of the surf-break.
We do watch the bobbing neighbours.
in the segregations of the bay.

Great Northern, *Loch a Tuath*

You've to look more than twice
to see what's in today.
That easterly must
sift and fetch
foodstuff but it gets trundled.

That's maybe why himself
is more down than up
till he steals a rise.
Bobbing on the surfer's wave,
dishevelled in silhouette,
more bulky than bonny
till the clean light hits the white
where a moderate neck meets
a wrestler's oxters and
high-contrast monochrome
rings out over distance

like a chequerboard sheer-strake –
top plank of the *sgoth Niseach* –*
built for such waters and
which you have to hope
will forever be
more up than down.

* *traditional craft of North Lewis*

Seilebost

The sandstream
sent by storm
hangs out in the air,
more plume than puff,
nothing like smoke.

About as steady as
the failing fenceline –
a severed stob,
suspended on rylock,
wavering a good way
from the vertical.

Up the slope, the
past pour of
concrete and pebbles
wisely set on rock –
gables solid as ever.
Angus says –
Back in the day
the mason took just one look
at the pile of stones,
gathered to throw
a bit of body
into the shuttering.

'Aye that might be about a third
of what we're going to need.'
That man's walls still look
on the level
from our angle.
Consistent skews

at his roof's edges,
unwavering though
the slates have flown.
The sarking's naked.
'The sale's gone through.
If the guy from away
gets his planning permission,
it's for demolition.'

We need people if
they really come to live
but I pity their chisels.

Can the stuff of our founds
increase at each casting
as the number of the sheltered
falls at each improvement?
How long, how high, how wide,
how deep and from just how far away
can we take and shift
while the tent-lines flood
faster than a Solway tide.

Solway Firth tide – 'faster than horse and rider', so we were told at primary schools

skews – slant or angle but also stone or concrete slabs at roof gable-ends to hold down slate edges

east, west, east coasts

Salmon-netters, Balmedie

Alkaline avalanche
of specks
amassing in mounds
soon to be broadcast –
grains make air visible.

Surf accelerates
at the gradient.
Clouds shed weight
to increase backwash.

This shore fair shifts.
Above suds, light splits
to a spectrum.
Not there for long.

Grit goes to the roots
of our hair and into ears
to wake epiphany
sharp as a stab –

the men in white seaboots *
reclining on the trailer –
smoko
between their tides.

An anchor or three,
actual but oxidised.
The staked-out nets
are holes or memory.

There's the coble –
plonked in the carpark,
painted up
but not for protection.

There's no going back to how it was
but you've got to pose the question –
Why should the devil
have all the best dunes?

*from a painting by Donald Smith

Balmedie, north of Aberdeen is a site of special scientific interest due to fluid wetlands as habitat.

Aberdeen council refused planning permission for the Trump golf course but this was overturned by the then Scottish Government. Subsequent expansions were approved despite a record number of protests.

The documentary films 'You've Been Trumped' and 'You've Been Trumped Too' by Anthony Baxter portray the local residents who would not sell out to corporation – members of the same Forbes family are subjects of the painting.

Eardley at Catterline *

Sea doesn't play fair.
En plein-air – doesn't cut it–
the least of the easterly is
a ballistic broadcast of chuckiestanes
sent at Joan's narrowed eyes.
She swats the finings
into her fluency
strokes it all in fast.
She might not be tied to a mast
or a rack of bagnets but
her easel is hobbled.

The sea-seed is in her shore.
Don't think all the waves have broken.
A wall, a cliff might give.
They might come at us.

* from a painting in The Hunterian collection

Peploe to Cadell *

How can you navigate
without knowing it?
How can you be underway but
keel-side up?

But we did sail, through June
from Peploe to Cadell.
Ardalanish shining astern
till we took the dog-legs through
pink to green granite –
Erraid to the Sound of Iona.

Clouds very like the islands under them
disorientate
as we reach, close, fine, free,
tack to tack till
we were looking up and out that other way
to shale and slate in the low stratus
inches over
or under
Loch na Keal.

*from two paintings in The Hunterian collection

Whistler in The Hunterian

It's what you can nearly see –
the hull under suggested sailcloth,
the fan of fingers, a fan itself,
the hem over bulge of boot.
You get the stances.
You wonder at the not-quite-red,
flower or pom or what
is left in the figure's wake –
a possibility of glow
out of scrupulous charcoal.

His own portrait – another arrangement
but can the self really be
skinny as a waif in a long coat?
Something like a reveal
in his organisation of
legs, arms, miraculous hands.

In The Hunterian

1.   Fish-hooks

A pibroch of Arctic variations
in the hinged barbs of fish-hooks
aye ready to snare on impact.

Down a hemisphere to
fixed but compound curves
in Polynesian solutions.

All examples cased
or you might say trapped
in our time.

The achieved shapes
various as ballads
sung over borders.

2.   Patents

Feet on mezzanine,
you can just about believe
a trace of the pulsing aorta

of meeting oceans
can be trapped in dots
in the tickertape you can feed

to a calibrated cog
within the brass and glass
of a prototype by Kelvin

numbered.

Arnish man

A purse with no coins
stockings with plenty darns
                        but no shoes.

How much patching can a man of 24
carry, in his own lifespan?

We walk the stories on
but his walk, his story
                        swung short
                        as the arc of a rock.

The undershirt, repair on repair,
of unsigned provenance.

A spoon of horn holds on,
its crack held by four rivets.

A brace of quills,
species not determined.

A short comb of bone,
the fine span and the quick
                        separated.

The casting-off
like a signature
in the hand-stitched bonnet.

His outergarment
so well made but

a single button out of eleven
repositioned

on a band of soft stripes
– into the only pocket.

A darker addition
on the right shoulder
and still more signs of strain.

The weavers of materials,
stitchers of artefacts –

also persons unknown –
their own bones will be jelly

but maybe at rest
as victim and perpetrator
must walk on or wait.

*Artefacts from circa 1700s, found with human remains in a shallow moor-
land grave, were returned to Lewis in 2025.*

On the Gower Peninsula

A lot of it's to do with
where you're perched –
pitch and toss on deck or
the dizzy stance
you settle to
on the green, green grass, not home.

These tide-range lengths of beach
look like a softish landing, from high
but I'm remembering signs of shallowing –
shifting shapes of waters in the bight
before numbers tumbled on the sounder
and the first hints of roar.

But I've come out on the service bus,
out of Swansea, the BBC
and the Dylan Thomas museum
so the only slightly absurd
theatre of lyricism in the dark
stays in the head until
headlights roam out
from the turning-point at Rhossili.
The driver speaks of bones of wood
uncovering then buried again.

There was only the two of us and
we didn't speak further but
I think we both maybe had a sense
of something like immensity –
not only in the gradient of the fall.

Tideway, Rathlin Sound
(for the late Russel Stewart)

Nothing's black and white, the warning goes,
but those hexagonals of Fair Head shine
dark. Offshore greys rip to bright shreds
till ribbons look like clans of eider
and also moan in camp comedy
as The Irish Sea empties
this way, a westerly curving flood
against the general grain
with a baroque range of variations
all yet bound to the moon.

Our vessels must also be contrary –
no keel on a currach – but
the nylon millimetres will bob pitch
like the tough feather
that is our frame as long
as oak straps, in compression,
are tense as a sniffing Rathlin hare –
as long as the slowing Gulf Stream sets
about northeast
about half a knot
not yet disrupted
by a swollen brackish rise
that mocks our notion of a norm.

Lines for Gerry Loose

Botanic Gardens, Glasgow, May 25, 2025
(first 3 lines from Ken Cockburn, renga master)

sense of presence
sense of absence
dandelions

surface rippled pimpled
in an absent breeze

something like a circle
leaves in a-breeze-and-a-half
couple of greens on mulch

solid foundations for nothing
light, shoots, bullet to sky

Seaflower of Ardnamurchan
ashore, afloat, in season
a low blow fair sweeps

friendship fires from dust
kaki and Scots pine

seeking more than reaping
willows coorie, huddle
quiet dragonflies spit

a foot, a n other
any order you like

pibroch variations
a leaf from the book of birds
inexact refrains

we say 'present' again
no-one says 'absent'

Shakin briggie

Oer i shakin briggie
aince mair atween
i Hebrides an i Norlan See
an a the watters
is steamin wi caul
as shairp as piked weir.
Icemelt meetin up
wi air thats jist tae damned warrm.

An am mindin Glenfeshie
wi olacs cast lik chuckiestanes
fae a day ayont imaginin.
I clockie has birled an
i verynear roon warld
is gey close tae crackin agin.

Dinna ken fit wy
a heid birls but
noo am mindin
an aulder wy o
ma faithers speakin –

we maun be
i sauf keepin
this ae nicht.

shakin briggie — suspension-bridge
piked weir — barbed wire
olacs— boulders (Gaelic origins)

Acknowledgements

Grateful thanks to editors and publisher of periodicals where many of these poems first appeared, sometimes in different versions:

Acumen
The Cafe Review, (Maine, USA), ed. Steve Luttrell
The Edinburgh Review
Magma (Islands edition, guest editors Niall Campbell, Fiona Moore, Safia Kamaria)
Northwords Now
The Poets' Republic
Poetry Scotland
Prospect (Australia), guest-editor Pete Hay
The Rialto
Transnational literature (Australia), guest-editor Alison Flett
Stand

Others appeared in the following anthologies:

'The Leaves of All the Years' – *Essays and Memories in William Neil's Centenary Year*, Drunk Muse Press, ed Hugh Macmillan, 2019

'The Earth Is Our Home' World Poetry Movement in association Mythic Horse Press and Playspace Publications, ed Gerry Loose, 2022

Scotia Extremis – Poems from the Extremities of Scotland's Psyche, ed Brian Johnstone and Andy Jackson, Luath Press, 2019

Dead Good Scots, ed Hugh Macmillan, Rocandora Press, 2021

Words from an Island, ed Meg Bateman, Skye Reading Room, 2013

Hunter's Voices, ed Alan Riach, Stewed Rhubarb, 2024

Thanks also to following projects/exhibitions where poems were developed (in order of appearance here):

Lyrics from 'Malin Hebrides, Minches' set to music by Diethelm Zuckmantel, Düsseldorf, from 1983

'Five fish' with the music of David P Graham, performed and published in Bonn and Cologne

Triangle Trust, Scottish Islands residencies, 2003–4

'Mactotem' exhibition and catalogue, *an Lanntair*, 1998

'One Clear Line' (with Pat Law, Norman Chalmers) Scottish Poetry Library, 2006

Commonwealth Poets United, Scottish Poetry Library / Edmonton Poetry Festival, 2014: : thanks to Robyn Marsack, Louise Halfe

Australian Wooden Boat Festival, 2015: thanks to Desiree Fitzgibbon and Tasmanian artists community

TRACS Scotland, Andy Hunter Bursary, Helen Anderson for assistance Iceland voyage, 2025

'Is a Thing Lost' multi-partner exhibition and publication supported by Creative Scotland, 2010–11

'residue – rock, word, wire' with photography of Colin Myers, paintings and artist's book by Christine Morrison, Comunn Eachdraidh Nis and Taigh Chearsabhagh, 2024

Ullaverse, exhibition curated Lorraine Thompson, 2021

Kater Murr's Press, Kasti Series ed David Miller, 2023